And Then There Were Stories ... Lessons from a Lifetime of Leadership

And Then There Were Stories ... Lessons from a Lifetime of Leadership

John R. Fall

DEDICATION

This book is dedicated to the men and women who, by their example, taught me everything I know about leadership, especially to my wife, Pilar (Nena), a professional Watercolorist, who looks at the world through an artist's eyes and continues to amaze and inspire me.

CONTENTS

Forward

This book is a collection of stories I've used over the years in speeches to small and large groups of people. A number of them asked if I could write the stories down, because they wanted to use the stories themselves and couldn't remember them.

Most of the stories are based upon my real-life professional experiences travelling all over the world as a senior global executive management leadership consultant working with organizations of all sizes. But many of the lessons I learned in life have come from seemingly ordinary people in some very ordinary circumstances, so I've included some of these stories as well.

Both humorous and insightful, the stories include some unusual experiences with entrepreneurs ("The Statue of Liberty Syndrome," "Give Him a Raise"), some lessons from my leadership consulting engagements with global corporations ("You're Trying to Put Your Children Through College; I'm Trying to Feed Them," "What Keeps You Up at Night?"), and a fascinating account of how my wife got her US citizenship ("They Were Patient With Their Lives").

The stories are all true, and in most instances I've even used the real first names of the people involved. After all, if it weren't for these extraordinary people this book would never have been written.

I've added stories to the original edition published in 2011 rather than publish a sequel. I hope you enjoy them.

Next Time, Try Working a Little Smarter

I worked my whole life, starting in grade school. And even though I am now semi-retired, I'm still working. I guess that's why I have little patience with people who complain about their situation in life, but haven't made any effort to better themselves.

I grew up in St. Louis, Missouri, in the heart of the Midwest in the United States. It was back in the 1950's, when all we had was black and white television -- if we had one at all -- and we got our news mostly from reading newspapers. We didn't know about the internet or email and had to use a phone booth if we wanted to make a telephone call while we were away from home or work.

But we had a work ethic that was taught not only at home, but also in school, and was ingrained in the culture.

My elementary school sponsored a summer camp each year for everyone in third grade. And, since this was a public school with people from all different incomes, everyone who wanted to go to the camp had to sell greeting cards to pay for it.

Yes, the rich kids could cheat by selling mostly to their parents and relatives, and, indeed some of them did. But most were honest and made an effort to sell to people they didn't know.

I didn't have to worry about those conflicts because we weren't rich.

My father loaned me his briefcase – which looked more like a suitcase – and I loaded it up with samples and I started going door to door in the neighborhood. Many of the people I met were already familiar with me because I had started a business of cutting their grass, so I had a built-in clientele for my new enterprise. I was pretty proud of myself, until one day when I was walking from one house to another, a group of kids a few years older started to taunt me.

"What are you doing?" they sneered. "Selling something or running away from home?"

I felt like crawling into the sidewalk but the cracks weren't that big. As luck would have it, my next prospect was already at the door, and she was someone I knew because she was one of my lawn mowing customers. She took one look at the other kids, and said loudly to them "Get out of here, and don't come back until you learn to be polite."

"Johnny," she said, "I don't know what you're selling but I'm sure I need it. And, I'll take extra."

I made my quota that day, and went on to sell more greeting cards than had ever been sold before by anyone in the school. It was a good lesson about persistence and I took it to my next job, selling newspapers.

There was a busy corner between my school and my house, where a lot of cars passed, and, on their way home, many of the people in the cars would stop and buy a newspaper. I went by there each day on my way home, until one day there was a man with a stack of newspapers who looked harried. "Hey kid," he shouted at me, "how would you like to make some money?"

It turned out he had a route of selling newspapers on street corners and the paper boy for that corner had just quit.

To make the opportunity even better, there was a White Castle hamburger stand right on the same corner. At the time, they were one of the premium places to get a hamburger. I don't know if they still have hamburger stands, but I know they are still in business because I found packaged frozen White Castle hamburgers in a supermarket in the Philippines.

If you are a fan of American hamburgers you owe it to yourself to try one. They are very small but unbelievably tasty hamburgers and you can eat several of them before you fill up.

So I was in the newspaper business. And it went very well for quite a while, that is, until the weather changed and it started to rain.

One day it rained for hours. I stood there in the driving rain, thinking people would feel sorry for me and buy more newspapers. It didn't work. They didn't even notice me; the rain was coming down too hard and all they wanted was to get home to their families where it was warm and dry. They decided if they wanted to learn what happened that day they could watch the news on television and forgo the newspaper.

I stood there in the rain and the cold, trying to elicit sympathy and sell some newspapers, until I couldn't stand it anymore. Even though I had been able to resist the smell of the hamburgers during the good weather, and brave the storm for a while when the weather turned bad, the temptation of the warmth inside the hamburger stand, combined with the smell of the hamburgers, was finally too much.

Wouldn't it be a nice ending if I told you the people in the White Castle took pity on me, and told me to relax and get warm?

Yes, it would be nice, but that's not what happened. Instead they said, "Hey, kid, this place is for paying customers only. So order up and pay up or get out." I ordered several hamburgers, french fries, and a chocolate milk shake. After all, I was just a kid and had a big appetite after standing in the cold and rain for a few hours. Of course, the rain stopped shortly after I placed my order and paid for it, but it didn't matter to me. I just waited inside in the warmth where I was dry until my order was ready.

I never had anything taste so good. But, I missed a lot of sales, and, as luck would have it, my boss came by and saw me inside sitting on the stool eating my hamburger, and that was the end of my career as a newspaper boy.

But before he let me go, my boss gave me some advice that I carried with me forever. He first asked me what happened, so I told him the story. He said, "Johnny, I've got a quota to make and my boss won't make any exceptions, so I'm sorry but I have to let you go. But, next time, work a little smarter instead of harder and you'll come out OK."

The advice stayed with me, and so did the memory of the hamburgers. They're still the best hamburgers I ever tasted.

I was never an athlete. Oh, I could swim OK, to the point that I was even a lifeguard for a day. But I was never good enough to be competitive. I played some sandlot baseball and was on the church softball team where they had to take anyone who showed up, because that's what you did for recreation if you grew up in St. Louis, Missouri in the US in the 1950's, but I never even got on the high school team.

But I found out I could sing -- not well enough to be a professional, but enough to be part of the choir and some other singing groups in high school, and to get some small parts in the school's operettas.

If you were in Hollywood in the US and trying to cast the part of a music teacher in a movie, you probably would have picked my high school music teacher, Miss Meyer. Miss Meyer was very tall and wore large horn-rimmed glasses. And she was extremely thin; we used to kid that if she stood sideways outside she wouldn't have a shadow.

She also had the worst set of false teeth I've ever heard. That's right, I said heard, because when she talked they would clack together and it was sometimes hard to understand her. But she had an ear for music and that's all she needed. She could pick out the one person -- or the several individuals one at a time -- who were slightly off-key out of the almost one hundred people in the choir.

She played the piano when we practiced, and had a metronome so we would have something to help us try to stay on beat. A better word for played is hammered. She really knew how to hit the keys. But I suppose if you try for decades to take a raucous group of high school students and get them to sing together you have to have some place to take out your frustration, and it's safer to hammer the piano keys than hammer the students. And, of course, don't forget she had the clamoring false teeth as an accompaniment as well.

Miss Meyer would work with one section of the choir at a time. She would find out which section sang the best and work with them first, usually either the sopranos or the altos because the girls were always better behaved and, for the most part, better singers than the boys.

Then she would work with either the tenors or the basses, whichever group provided less frustration.

And we would sing the same phrases, over and over, until they actually started to sound pretty good. Pretty good, that is, until the groups started to sing at the same time and then chaos reigned for a while.

But, eventually, after a few months of practice, the sounds started to blend. And, only then, Miss Meyer let us know about the performance. We were going to sing in front of the whole school. So, immediately after she let us know about this we all fell apart and she had to put us back together again

But she'd done this before, and was extremely patient and persistent, and knew how to tweak us. She would start with the individual sections, and put them together one by one until some real music started to come out.

And she would always pause, and say "Now, let's put it all together" and we would start singing from the beginning. And, somehow magically, that's what would happen; we were able to put it all together and sound like we knew what we were doing.

It was much later when I remembered the phrase and started to use it in my consulting. It's amazing how effective it is, no matter what you are trying to orchestrate.

He was larger than life, and, without a doubt, the best salesman I ever knew. Everyone called him Bob, but we called him Dad.

We lived in St. Louis, Missouri, in the middle of the US. But for as long as I can remember we visited my uncle every summer in San Diego, California on the Western Southernmost coast of the Pacific Ocean in the US.

We didn't have enough money to air condition our car so we drove across the desert at night when the heat was at least bearable. I can still remember waking up in the back seat of the car and hearing the construction workers repairing the roads. I guess the daytime sun was too much for them too.

My father eventually gave up his position as Vice President of an oil additive company in St. Louis and became a manufacturer's representative for several different companies with an eclectic mix of products including decals, office machine shredders and some others so he could move to San Diego and enjoy the wonderful weather and the sound of the Pacific Ocean.

My mother was a Registered Nurse and it was her salary that kept us afloat until my father started his advertising business in the spare room of a gas station owned by a friend – a business that prospered to the point that my mother could retire from nursing.

My parents are both gone, and my brother, Don, runs the business today and, even though he's now of retirement age, he loves it so much he still continues to work.

There are a number of stories that I could relate about my father but this is one of my favorites.

I was in college and had moved out of the family home – something quite common in the US even though it's an idea that is still foreign if you're in Asia. But I visited my family often and loved to hear my father's stories.

He was very successful in his business and, at the time, the automobile that every successful person bought was a General Motors Cadillac. In fact, he was so successful he bought a new one every year. And, being the salesman that he was, he knew it was better if he sold the old one himself rather than trade it in at the dealers.

So, imagine my surprise when, some months later, there were still two Cadillac's in the driveway – the new one and the unsold old one.

I asked him if he decided not to sell the old one. He answered with a grin, "No, everybody decided not to buy."

I thought about that comment years later when I was consulting with senior executives. Every one of them told me that you couldn't beat consumer perception; it's why their organizations spent so much on advertising and promotion and market research.

And I finally understood that my father had just been the victim of a changing market – a market where the US made automobiles no longer were the symbol of success. The European brands had succeeded them.

So, remember that you constantly need to be aware of consumer perception, or, you too will be someday faced with the words "Everybody decided not to buy."

Ralph was an expert with an oscilloscope. They don't use them much anymore so you may not even know what it is. Today they have streamlined computer repair to replacing circuit boards from a central repair depot. But back then, you hooked an oscilloscope up to the innards of the computer and it would display enough information on a small green screen about the flow of electrons within the circuit board so an expert could not only make a correct diagnosis but could fix the problem.

Such was the state of the art in the 1960's when I joined IBM and first learned about how computers worked. They didn't teach anything about computers in the schools back then so I had to go to work before I could learn. I was in San Diego, California in the Southwest portion of the United States and had just graduated from college with a Mathematics and English major.

I was the President of the Mathematics Club and needed a speaker for a meeting. We were all interested in finding out more about computers and decided it would be great if we could find someone who could tell us what was happening. One of the largest organizations in the computer business at the time was IBM so I called and asked if they had anyone who could come speak to us.

IBM had a reputation at the time for being pretty stuffy – three piece suits with white shirts and striped ties and wing tipped shoes were the uniform that everyone wore. So we were pretty pleasantly surprised when the speaker showed up. Even though Larry wore the "uniform" he drove a fire engine red MG sports car, wore the brightest red bow tie we'd ever seen, and gave us a great introduction to what was happening with computing at the time.

It was such a good speech that a few months later, when I was about to graduate, I decided to apply for a job with IBM as a Systems Engineer. Before I got hired I had to pass a number of tests including a psychological test, as well as a number of interviews.

After all of that I considered myself extremely lucky to get the job. It was only much later I found out that IBM was so hungry for good people that Larry was given a set of golf clubs in appreciation for finding me.

Since I didn't have any computer education at all, the first thing IBM did was send me to Dallas, Texas in the Midwest in the US, which was over a thousand miles away, for a ten week basic training class. They taught me about computers, programming, operating systems and how to make presentations. Imagine all of this in ten weeks. I'm sure you can guess how little I really knew when I graduated from their basic training.

But fortunately Ray, the IBM branch manager, was a seasoned executive who had moved to San Diego from Pittsburgh, Ohio to get out of the winter months before he retired and knew how to manage the new folks.

He put me into General Dynamics, an aerospace firm, along with a number of other experienced IBM people where I couldn't get into too much trouble, even though I didn't know how to do very much.

It was an exciting time. IBM's operating systems weren't working and they had bet the future of the company on their success. This was way before Microsoft and Apple and Google and other companies you hear about today.

So I had the opportunity, right out of college with no more computer education than the basic ten week school, to debug the operating system programming and help implement some fixes to it.

It turned out the computer hardware didn't work much better than the software so it was always in need of repair. And that's how I met Ralph.

When it came to the difficult problems they always gave them to Ralph. But Ralph was not without problems of his own. He really enjoyed partying, especially on the weekends, and Chuck, his manager, could pretty much count on getting a call from Ralph about once a month on a Friday night around one in the morning, asking Chuck to come down and bail him out of jail, where the police who also got to know Ralph put him to keep him out of trouble.

Ralph also had a habit of wearing red socks. It didn't matter what color suit he had on, – and remember even the hardware repair people wore the IBM uniform – Ralph thought he needed a little color. Combined with his ability to fix difficult problems that no one else could fix, it earned Ralph the nickname of Superman because they said he had his Superman suit on under his IBM uniform.

One Friday night – actually Saturday morning around two AM – Ralph was at work trying to diagnose a difficult problem and not having much luck. Fortunately, it was a Friday night when Ralph hadn't partied too much, and was available to help solve the problem.

Phil, the customer's third shift manager, was new, and under pressure to keep things on a schedule that was falling further and further behind, so he kept interrupting Ralph and asking him when the problem would be solved.

Ralph put up with about three interruptions before he exploded.

"It'll be fixed sooner if you quit asking when," he shouted at the manager and went back to his work.

Phil turned enough shades of red to match Ralph's Superman suit, stormed off back to his office and called Chuck.

Chuck, like Ray, was a seasoned executive and was waiting for the call. He knew Ralph and he also knew Phil was new.

"Phil," Chuck said, "Ralph is the best technician I have. But he needs to concentrate. He may not have the best political skills, and I apologize for the outburst, but in this case he's right.
Leave him alone and pretty soon your computers will be running again."

Phil protested some more but knew it was in vain. He left Ralph alone, and sure enough, before long everything was fixed.

So the next time you are tempted to ask someone when something is going to be fixed, remember Ralph, and leave the fixer alone to do their job. It will probably take less time.

NAMES ARE POWERFUL

I owe this one to Ray, the Branch Manager of IBM in San Diego, California in the US. I was fresh out of college in my first job, and because of my outgoing personality my manager tried to turn me into a salesman. But I think it had more to do with IBM's need for salesmen than my ability.

I tried it for a while, but it wasn't what I wanted to do; I was happy as a Systems Engineer, a more technical position, and when I told my manager I wanted to go back to doing what I knew best I was certain I was going to lose my job all together and maybe even lose my chance for a career.

But I was lucky. Ray knew people and he took me out to breakfast to reassure me that everything was OK. "Johnny," he said, using a nickname I hadn't heard since I was a kid, "don't worry. We need your talents wherever you decide to stay. And you might even change your mind later."

I didn't change my mind, but I never forgot how I was treated. So the next time you promote someone who doesn't really want to be promoted, think about Ray, and be certain you don't lose a valuable asset for your organization.

And speaking of nicknames, I've learned they really differ depending upon the culture. In the US we tend to use diminutives like Johnny instead of John that disappear as we mature.

But in the Philippines, where my wife was born, the childhood nicknames never go away. You'll find grown up Senators called "Boy" and "Bong." And Russian novels are famous for multiple names that turn out to be the same person. So when you use a person's name, make certain you understand the culture.

The best book I ever read about the power of names was Dale Carnegie's classic "How to Win Friends and Influence People." If you haven't read it you owe it to yourself to find a copy. Ray was savvy enough to know that to me the nickname was endearing as well as powerful. So don't be afraid to use whatever name you are used to using with your employees; they'll appreciate your candor.

If You Have To Have An Answer Today, The Answer is "NO"

John was a banker who got in on the ground floor of computer leasing in the US. It was a long time ago, back in the late 1960's. The government had been after IBM for years, threatening to break it up as a monopoly. T.J Watson Jr. preempted his father, the founder of IBM, and signed a Consent Decree with the US government because he knew they were in a position to carry through on their threat to break up the organization.

Prior to the signing of the Consent Decree, IBM did not sell their mainframe computers; they only leased them. Along with the lease they bundled in a variety of services that made it difficult for others to compete.

As part of the Consent Decree, IBM agreed to sell their computers. Several companies sprung up overnight. They bought the computers from IBM, and leased them at very competitive rates to organizations that had previously leased from IBM.

Many of the leasing companies were founded by banks, and while the banks knew all about how to finance and make money, they didn't know anything about how to lease computers.

The smart ones hired away Marketing Managers from IBM, who already had the contacts needed to break into the large companies and institutions that were the prime targets for leasing the mainframe computers. To be able to hire them away they gave them a great deal of money, and made them all Vice Presidents of the new organization. They knew you had to really be important to become a Vice President of IBM and most of the folks understood they would never reach that level.

It turned out to be the start of my consulting business. As a Systems Engineer for IBM, I was trained in supporting the mainframe computers, and well respected by everyone, especially

Hugh, the Marketing Manager that got hired away. So when Hugh went into the computer leasing business he brought me along as a technical consultant.

I flew all over the Western United States, providing the technical support required during the sales and installation cycles of the large computers.

I flew so much, in fact, that for a while, the only place that felt like home was the front cabin of an aircraft. That's right, even back then they had frequent flyer programs and I flew enough that I almost always ended up in a free First Class seat. It was back in the days before all the security we have to deal with today, so you could run down the halls of the airport to catch a plane at the last minute, and even write your own ticket and hand it to the stewardess after you boarded the plane. I must admit that I miss that part of travel while I wait in the long lines and take off my shoes and belt, to make the travel safe.

In addition to working with customers, I was able to attend and sometimes add information to the management meetings. It was an eclectic mixture of people at the meetings. Headed by John, the banker that founded the organization, each meeting also consisted of the Vice Presidents for the four regions in the United States; who were former Marketing Managers with IBM and typical very aggressive salesmen.

In those days the way to succeed at IBM was to spend part of your time selling to prospects and part of your time with your management getting your quota reduced. This held true not only for the salespeople but also for the Marketing Managers.

So they all thought that this same technique would work in the new organization, and part of each meeting was always a push by one or more of the new Vice Presidents to get something from John. For quite a while John would listen attentively; he knew he needed the expertise of the people he hired, so he was always polite. And he was usually patient, until one day when one of the Vice Presidents just wouldn't give up. He asked for a concession, was told by John that he would think about it, and in a few minutes asked again ... and again ... and again ... until John finally lost patience and told him "If you have to have an answer today, the answer is 'NO'!"

The room got quiet, and the meeting ended. So did the employment of the Vice President who wouldn't give up. John had finally had enough. After that, everyone picked up the expression and would use it on the salesmen they hired.

You might try using it yourself; it's unbelievably effective. In fact, try it on your children. I guarantee you they will understand, even if they pretend at first not to.

My first new client after the computer leasing business taught me more about management, even though I was still technical. It's where I met Dan. Dan was the Data Processing Manager (that was the title before we got sophisticated and called it Information Technology and invented the Chief Information Officer – CIO – position) at a firm that manufactured a device that made it easier for supermarket personnel to reorder their stock.

It was way before the scanners that we see everywhere today in supermarkets and retail stores. The store manager went around all of the shelves in the supermarket, and when he determined they needed something, recorded the order on a sheet of paper. This was a daunting task, as most supermarkets had over 10,000 different items.

So, along came the first electronic device. It was unbelievably primitive by today's standards. The engineers tapped off the keys of a large adding machine and recorded the keystrokes on a small tape recorder. To power the device and make it portable, they used a car battery, and put everything on a large cart that the store manager wheeled around the supermarket.

When the order was complete, the store manager dialed a number at the computer center. When he heard a high-pitched tone, he placed the phone in a device called an acoustic coupler, and, at an unbelievably slow speed, transmitted the order to headquarters.

The story gets even better. At headquarters was a device that received the electronic order and punched a paper tape. The paper tape was then put into another device that read the paper tape and punched 80-column cards.

Finally, the cards were fed into a mainframe computer, where a program processed the order.

If I've lost you along the way, don't worry. I think you get the idea of how primitive this was.

What's the best part of the story? They made millions -- in 1960's US dollars. And they hired me, as a Systems Engineer, to help make this clumsy process work.

It turned out to be a wonderful learning experience in management, which made up for the lack of technology. We had to coordinate a large number of resources, some in the computer department and some in the store and, yes, even back then they all hated each other.

We had to train the store personnel to put labels on the shelves with the number and name of the product, so they could easily know what to punch into the adding machine for reordering. We had to help the computer people write the programs necessary to take in the orders, eliminate the problems with them, and alert the warehouse of the items that needed to be replenished. We had to coordinate this with the stores that were still using the old way to order, until we could finally get everyone to use the new way.

But let's go back to my friend Dan. Dan knew I thought the technology was crude, but he also knew I was overlooking the management lessons. He took me out to dinner one night, listened to my complaints, smiled and told me I was missing the whole point.

"John," he said. "As you move along in your career, you won't care so much about the technology. You will learn that it's getting the people motivated and coordinated that's the hard part and also the part that means the most. You need to quit using the mathematical part of your brain where you think in formulas.

Let me tell you about one of my programmers -- Bob. Bob is absolutely brilliant; you can give him any technical challenge and he will solve it in a surprisingly elegant way.

But Bob is a maverick, and he'll work on things that he thinks are important, instead of what you ask him to do.

I came in early one morning, and there was Bob; he was unshaven, in a wrinkled shirt, with bleary eyes, and a huge grin on his face. 'Look, Dan' he exclaimed, 'at what I was able to do last night!'

It was indeed brilliant but, unfortunately, wasn't what I had asked him to do. And we had a management presentation that day to the President and all the Vice-Presidents.

I finally lost my temper, and told him: 'Bob, this isn't my birthday, I don't need any surprises'.

He looked at me with a light of revelation in his eyes and said 'Why didn't you put it that way before? Now I get it.'

And, from that time on, Bob always worked on my priorities first, and his second.

Remember this, John; it's more important than any technological advance you'll ever make."

I can't tell you how many times I've used that story and that expression. I always share the story at the beginning of any project that I undertake. And, even though I have to remind the folks periodically, I get fewer and fewer surprises, except, of course, once a year on my birthday, when a surprise is welcomed.

WHAT CAN I DO?

If you're reading this book in order, you've already been introduced to Dan in the last story. If you're jumping around, don't worry, you don't need to read about Dan to understand this story. But be sure at some time to read "It's Not My Birthday ... I Don't Need Any Surprises." I'm certain you'll enjoy it and you'll see how much Dan has meant to me.

Not too long after I met Dan, his mother passed away. I don't know how many of you still have your mothers, but they are really special and if your mother is still alive be sure to tell her, if you haven't done so lately, how much you love her, and how much of what you are today is due to her kindness, love and guidance.

In Dan's case, though, this story revolves more around the millions of US Dollars that he inherited and what to do with it than the passing of his mother.

His mother had been very ill for quite a long time and, in some ways, it was a blessing for her finally to move on, away from the pain.

My wife and I had dinner with Dan, to see how he was doing and to pass along our sympathy.

After talking about his mother for quite a while, Dan told us about the inheritance.

"I always knew my mother had money," Dan said. "My father made quite a bit of money and my mother listened to him after he died about being sure to leave the accounts with a trusted money manager, so she not only preserved the capital, but really increased it."

"My problem is," he continued, "I don't know much about investing and the money manager is retiring and I'm not sure what to do now."

I'll bet you wish you had Dan's problem. I know my wife and I looked at each other and with the non-verbal communication that only comes from your trusted partner, knew what the other was thinking, which we confirmed later.

But then Dan continued, in typical Dan fashion, and said "But, I guess you're wishing you had my problem. And, it really doesn't matter that there are a lot of things that I can't do, and many things that I shouldn't do, what only matters is what CAN I do? And, I guess that's true about most things in life, not just this situation."

So Dan did what you might expect – he asked his long-time friend and CPA (Certified Public Accountant) for advice and took it, and last time we checked, like his mother, and his father before her, he continued the family tradition and he not only held onto the capital, but managed to really expand it.

And I've never forgotten the lesson I learned from Dan:

> As confused as we often get, it's not enough to just determine what our problems are. And it's certainly not enough to come up with a list of things that we CAN'T do. We have to always determine what we CAN do, and then immediately proceed to do it!

For another version of the same lesson, read on and find out what my client Gordon had to say.

It was in the early 1970's and I was just beginning my management consulting practice. I had been an excellent technician, and because of that, I got a number of referrals from many of my satisfied clients. Some were so enthusiastic they even talked about how they enjoyed my stories, and used them and the lessons they contained in their management.

That's how I met Gordon. Gordon had recently been promoted to General Manager of the San Diego, California US organization of a global manufacturing enterprise, and among the problems he was facing was pressure to adopt some software created by one of the larger organizations in the enterprise. Gordon was an excellent manager, which is why he had been promoted, but like many senior managers at the time, he had come up through the ranks on the engineering side and IT was new and somewhat unknown to him.

These days the senior executives I work with are fairly well versed in the role of IT -- especially since the world changed to acknowledge the business side of IT -- but at the time it was still a mystery to many people.

I used the same approach I use to this day in my consulting. I interviewed Gordon to obtain his perception of the problem. I then interviewed everyone involved to find out what they thought.

I summarized what I had discovered and prepared a written and verbal report for Gordon. In the report I outlined everything that had brought Gordon to the present condition, including the fact that Gordon couldn't use the software because his business was very different from the organization that had the software they were trying to get him to use.

Then I stopped, proud of the work that I had done, and asked Gordon what he thought. "John," he said, "you've done an excellent job of explaining what I CAN'T do, and I really appreciate your effort. However, you stopped too soon, because you haven't told me yet what I CAN do."

So I went back to the drawing board and expanded my report, explaining what Gordon needed to tell his management, including the fact that he needed funding to improve the software he was already using.

Gordon took my suggestions to heart, added his own touches, and was able to obtain the funding he needed.

And I've never forgotten the lesson I learned from Gordon. As confused as we often get, it's not enough to just determine what our problems are. And it's certainly not enough to come up with a list of things that we CAN'T do. We have to always determine what we CAN do, and then immediately proceed to do it!

Bob and Dick used to work for a large corporation that moved to a small town just north of San Diego, California in the US. Bob was the Executive Vice President and Dick worked for him as the Data Processing Manager. This was in the 1970's before the term Information Technology had been invented and there were no personal computers or mobile telephones, so in a way life was simpler then.

But life was much the same in large corporations and Bob and Dick decided they were more entrepreneurial so they went into business together.

They formed a new corporation and built up a good local business as a service bureau, offering computer services to small organizations in the area. They had a staff of keypunch operators and would get information from their customers that they would punch into cards and then feed them into computer programs they had written to produce billing and financial statements. Yes, it's the same type of thing we do today without the punched cards, and if you're not old enough to remember what punched cards were you're not missing anything.

It was a very successful business that generated enough profit that when one of their customers decided to put in a computer of their own Bob and Dick offered to help program it. Which is how I got involved. I still had technical skills at the time and found out through a friend that Bob and Dick needed some help.

They had become a distributor for a company that offered mid-range computers and had one young man working on programming the new system for their client.

It had turned out to be more complicated than they planned for and they had made the mistake of offering to program the new system at a fixed price.

If you're reading this book from front to back, instead of skipping around in the stories, you'll come across my story later titled "The Statue of Liberty Syndrome" where I talk more about my own experience with fixed price contracts.

And you'll find out I wasn't much better at it than Bob and Dick at the beginning. Thank goodness I got better.

So I helped Bob and Dick finish the new system for their client, and learned more from them than they probably learned from me.

I was new to project management and struggled along as best as I could at the time, but, looking back now, I realize I could probably do a better job today than I could then, but I guess we could all say the same about most everything we do.

I used to meet Bob and Dick once a week for breakfast at a small Mexican restaurant where we would have some of the best enchiladas I've ever eaten and discuss where we were on the project.

Bob and Dick had been having breakfast together once a week for a few years and it proved to be a very successful way to manage their business.

In addition to some of the more formal project management techniques and tools, it's still one of the best things I still retain today.

So instead of a formal meeting, you might try using the same technique. Try having a breakfast meeting instead.

It doesn't have to be a Mexican restaurant; choose the type of food that works for you and your group. But don't forget to socialize as well as cover the business topic.   You'll learn more than you might think and your people will never forget the experience.

If you're reading this book in order, you already met Bob and Dick in the last story. If you're skipping around, don't worry, here's who they are. Bob and Dick used to work for a large corporation that moved to a small town just north of San Diego, California in the US. Bob was the Executive Vice President and Dick worked for him as the Data Processing Manager. This was in the 1970's before the term Information Technology had been invented and there were no personal computers or mobile telephones, so in a way life was simpler then.

But life was much the same in large corporations and Bob and Dick decided they were more entrepreneurial so they went into business together.

They formed a new corporation and built up a good local business as a service bureau, offering computer services to small organizations in the area.

While there are many stories from Bob and Dick that I think you'd enjoy, this is one of my favorites and it came from Bob.

Before they were a large enough organization to be able to hire a salesman, Bob and Dick used to be the ones who would call on prospective and existing customers. And, during the conversations they would have, often the customer would say something that was, quite frankly, entirely foolish.

However, like all successful salesmen, they had learned the technique of never saying anything to irritate their customer.

So, after one customer said something that was obviously off the wall, Bob paused, stroked his chin and said "Makes you think."

The customer replied, "Yes, it certainly does." And then the conversation moved on to something more sensible.

Bob said he'd tried some more unsuccessful responses but nothing proved to be more effective.

So, next time your employee, customer, or even your spouse or children say something obviously inane, remember Bob's famous response and say "Makes you think."

I'm sure you'll find it much more effective than some of the more insulting responses and you can pretend it's your own.

Ed drove a huge Cadillac El Dorado convertible with a set of longhorns as a hood ornament and a horn that played "The Eyes of Texas are Upon You" when he blew it. Instead of a coffee table in his office, he had a roulette wheel covered with glass, and would take off the glass and challenge his visitors to gamble with him ... and almost always win. He was short, not quite five feet tall (about 1.5 meters), but he was one of those people that are truly larger than life. When I met Ed he had just moved to Southern California from Houston, Texas in the US.

I was consulting for a mortgage company. It was in the mid 1980's in the US and the industry was in trouble. Interest rates were shooting through the roof and home values were plummeting throughout the country. The problem was to be repeated decades later, only in far greater proportions, and lead to a worldwide recession.

Needless to say, it was difficult for them to get new business. In addition, large retail organizations like Sears had just started to offer mortgages through their retail outlets, and the small company I was working with was afraid if they didn't do something soon they would be unable to continue in business.

They looked into a variety of options, and, in the end, decided it was best to acquire a real estate franchise which would provide them an automatic source of new customers. It was at the time that the real estate franchise business was just starting to boom, so they felt they were getting in on the ground floor of something.

Unfortunately, they were in too much of hurry, and the company they bought contained a host of problems, including the president, who had used every shady trick in the book to build his company.

After not too long a time, they fired the president and went on a nationwide search for a new one. They enlisted a premier search agency to find their new president and the agency had managed to discover Ed.

Ed was well suited for the position. He had built up a successful real estate business in St. Louis, Missouri in the Midwest in the United States and sold it to the most successful of the large real estate franchising companies. As you'll soon see, in addition to the money he got for the business, he got some of the best advice he ever received.

Shortly after he sold his business Ed started having trouble selling real estate. It was a real problem for Ed, not only for his ego, but also because a large part of his profit in the sale of his business was based upon a complicated formula of how much new business he was able to bring in for the first three years after the sale.

Gil, the chairman of the real estate franchising business, flew in to meet with Ed. It was certainly not a social call. Gil spent three full days with Ed, first reviewing all of his plans and then attending sales meetings and working with Ed and individual salespeople as they tried to revive the business.

You'll read more about stress later but, trust me; no matter how much stress you think you have been under at any time in your life, it's nothing compared to what happened to Ed. He spent several sixteen to eighteen hour days of pure misery. Gil was not only relentless, he was obnoxious. He told Ed he couldn't believe how bad he was. He threatened to sue Ed and, not only take away all the money he had already given him for his business, but also add millions to the lawsuit for false representation.

At the end of the long third day, Gil said to Ed, "What's the most expensive restaurant in town?"

"The dining room of the Ritz Carlton," Ed replied immediately. "It's where I used to take all of my good clients to celebrate. My wife and I stayed there years ago on our honeymoon."

"Make us a reservation for dinner tonight," Gil ordered. "And call your wife and tell her to join us there. I've got some things to say and I want her to hear them as well."

Ed did as he was told and warned his wife, who had already heard the stories of what had been transpiring the last few days, to expect the worst.

Ed and his wife met Gil at the Ritz Carlton and held their breath, waiting for another tirade from Gil, but instead he was charming. He ordered champagne and caviar, and told stories of how he had built up his real estate franchising business.

Then he paused, and said "But, enough about me, that's not why I invited you here."

Ed and his wife thought, this was it, now the ax will drop and we'll find out how much trouble we are really in.

But, instead, Gil said, "Ed, you built up one of the most successful real estate businesses in the country. That's why I bought it. In the process, I'm sure you faced some unbelievably tough situations. What you are facing now is just another tough situation."

"What happened to you is you forgot who you are. So I've booked the Presidential Suite here for you and your wife at my expense. Treat it like a second honeymoon. There's only one thing I want you to promise me. Reminisce together about how you built your business. Remember the tough times and how you were able to get around them."

"I don't want to see you for another two days. And when I do I want the old Ed back."

It worked. And Ed never forgot it. I've used the advice myself as I faced tough situations and it has always worked for me. I'll bet it works for you too.

Marty was the antithesis of Ed. Where Ed was flamboyant, Marty was reserved. Where Ed was a spendthrift, Marty was frugal. Ed drove a Cadillac El Dorado Convertible and Marty drove a rebuilt MG sports car. Ed had a desk made out of a roulette wheel; Marty had a kidney-shaped wooden desk made out of plywood.

If you haven't already guessed, I'm talking about the same mortgage company as the last story. Marty was the Senior Vice President of Loan Servicing for the mortgage company and he was one of the best professional managers I've ever met.

I met Marty through a friend at IBM. I had maintained contact with many of the people I worked with before, and in this case it turned into business.

Marty had a small Information Technology department that he wanted to expand. They had developed their own software to service the loans because that's what you did at the time, and wanted to upgrade it along with some new software to originate the loans.

They had a mid-range computer and IBM had been trying to convince them they needed to upgrade to a mainframe computer but Marty wasn't convinced that was the right way to go, and asked his salesman Rene if he knew anybody that didn't work for IBM that could help him.

So that's how I got involved with the mortgage company. The first few meetings with Marty were interesting. I sat in Marty's office while he brought in a number of people, usually one at a time, but sometimes in groups, and we all just talked. We talked about the day to day problems and how they were going to handle them. We talked about sports and what was happening in the world. After a few days, Marty said to me, "John, you'd better reserve some time for us because we have a lot happening here and we'll need your advice."

Just like that I had a new client. We selected a few people from different parts of the organization and we all went to an IBM class together to learn about their new methodology "Business Systems Planning."

It was a straightforward way of coming up with Information Technology requirements for the organization and we ended up with a thick book that documented everything they needed.

We moved on from there into the second part of the consulting engagement. Marty realized he needed to build a completely new Information Technology department if he was going to be able to create the new software we had defined for the organization.

We searched first for a new department manager and found a wonderful fellow who had been with a small software firm that was in the process of going out of business. During the hiring process I helped Marty and everyone with the interviewing, and learned that the process Marty had used with me was his standard way of hiring senior advisors and employees.

We then hired a number of people from all over the US and succeeded in building systems that surpassed the capabilities of the packaged software available at the time. The whole process was so successful we even published an article about it in the premier magazine for the industry.

In addition to the mortgage company learning from me, I learned a lot from Marty.

Marty wanted to make certain whoever he brought in would not only have the right aptitude for the job, but also someone who would have the right attitude. He didn't want someone who would just defer to the other managers, but he also didn't want someone who would be so forceful they would demand their way all the time.

"John," Marty said, "we have been careful as we built this organization. We talked with a number of the major consulting firms about how to do it and, quite frankly, we didn't like their attitude. They treat people as interchangeable and expendable. I suppose they have to do it that way because of their size, but it doesn't mean we have to do the same thing. At least, not for now until we grow some more."

"We take care of our people, and we expect them to take care of us in return. We broke apart the jobs so people can perform different functions during the day. This way they don't get bored and we aren't incapacitated when someone is out."

"We have metrics for each job so we know everyone is being as productive as they should be. But the metrics aren't as important as taking care of our customers, so we don't measure each second someone is on the phone."

"We constantly meet with our employees and give them feedback and ask the same from them.

Everyone goes home at night fulfilled. It's so ingrained in our culture you'll find posters on each floor with that motto."

"And it has worked for us. Now you know why we were so careful hiring you. Your work has been instrumental in moving us into another plateau and we needed to make certain it would be done right, and with respect for each of our employees and future employees."

It's not a bad way to run your life. Everyone goes home at night fulfilled.

I CAN EARN THE MONEY BACK ... I CAN'T GET THE TIME BACK

I owe this story to Frank. He's the consultant from IBM in Atlanta, Georgia in the US who helped me with IBM's Business Systems Planning study at the mortgage company I mentioned in the last story.

Frank travelled all over the US with his consulting and held us spellbound with some of his stories.

One of my favorites is a story about a presentation he made to the managers of large industrial plants all over the world. He kept referring to one of the managers as "Rick, the largest plant manager in the world."

The audience got very quiet when Rick stood up and corrected Frank's English, saying "Frank, I know I've gained weight since we've met, but not that much! I think you meant to say I was the manager of one of the largest plants in the world, and as far as I know that's probably still true."

After a short pause you could hear the chuckles in the audience and everyone relaxed. To this day I still suspect that Frank said it wrong on purpose. But, regardless if it was deliberate or a mistake it certainly was effective.

I think that's why Frank was so engaging; he never hesitated to tell stories on himself.

But the story with the message I remember the most is about the large bank that was using IBM's Business Systems Planning to help modernize their antiquated systems. It was a multi-million US$ project and Frank was speaking to Jim -- the President of the organization -- to make certain he understood the scope of the effort.

"Frank," Jim said in his Southern US drawl, "we don't really have a choice. Yes, I know it's expensive. But it's an investment not just an expense. You see, I can earn the money back. It's why I'm here. But I can't get the time back. Our competitors are already way ahead of us. If we don't get this done right and done quickly we'll be out of business!"

It's food for thought, no matter what business you're in. And it's a message that applies to your personal life as well. So quit procrastinating and face that tough situation you've been avoiding and make the decision you've been putting off. You'll never find a better time than now and it will become your new way of life. It's what separates the ordinary from the extraordinary.

It was in the 1980's and I was looking for business, so I placed an advertisement in a nationwide computer newspaper. It's what you did at the time. The internet and CNN and news on mobile phones weren't here yet so people still read things printed on paper.

It was a small advertisement that basically said "If you need help and it's something to do with Information Technology, you should call me."

To my surprise, some months after I ran the advertisement the phone rang. It was from someone in a construction company in South Carolina in the US, clear across the country from where I lived in Southern California.

The call was from Rick, the President of a subsidiary of the construction firm. They had developed some software for the construction firm they thought they could sell all over the country. I talked with Rick for a while, and then said, "Well, it sounds like I can help. Send me a plane ticket and I'll come see what we can do together."

I knew I took Rick by surprise because there was a long pause, followed by some stammering, and then he said "well, I'll get back to you."

I went home that night pretty sure I'd never hear from Rick again. But two days later I got a call again. Rick wanted to know if it was OK if I paid for the trip and they reimbursed me.

I was expecting the call and knew how to handle it. "Rick," I said, "we don't know each other yet. We've talked on the phone and we've probably checked each other out. I see you have been in business for quite a while and, even though we are in the middle of a construction recession, your financials look OK.

I've given you some references and I know you've called some of them because they called me and told me you called.

But, we haven't really done any business together so how do I know that I'll get paid once I make the trip?

I'm not looking for an advance on my consulting fee, and if you aren't happy I won't even charge you for my time. All I want to know is that, if something goes wrong, it will just have cost me some time, not money."

Rick said he would get back to me. I went home again thinking I'd never hear from him again.

But I heard from him the next morning. He was all excited, and wanted to know when I could make the trip.

I told him I'd see him the next week and he assured me the ticket would be there for the plane trip.

Rick then explained what had happened. Rick explained he didn't have the authority to guarantee the ticket so he talked with Jim, the Financial Vice President of the construction firm. Jim was so tight with the company's money everyone was afraid of him.

"Rick," Jim said, the first time Rick asked for the money. "How do we know we don't have a 'Mon Back?"

I stopped Rick and said "You'll have to explain what that means. I've never heard the expression before."

So Rick explained that in the South it was a standard expression, and referred to one of the fellows who picked up the trash. It was the one who walked behind the trash truck, and when the truck went too far ahead he would say "'Mon Back", which meant come on back because you missed the trash cans.

"That's when I checked your references and went back to Jim again," Rick explained. "And he still wasn't satisfied.

I still don't like to part with the company's money with someone I've never met," Jim told me.

"I called you," Rick said, "and your explanation made sense to me. I decided it was worth one more conversation with Jim before I gave up.

'Well, finally, you've convinced me you found someone who knows what he is doing,' Jim proclaimed when I gave him your explanation. 'If this fellow is smart enough to make certain he's not stuck for a plane ticket he probably knows enough to help us.' I guess we don't have a 'Mon Back after all.'"

It was the start of an eight month engagement. I wish I could say the subsidiary was a huge success, but the story doesn't end that way.

It turned out the software they had invented wasn't professional enough. And there was another organization that had developed similar but much better software and was about to take their company public to provide them the financing they needed to expand.

In the end, I recommended they shut down the subsidiary and quit pouring good money after bad. They were grateful to hear the news, as they had pressing priorities for the money because the construction business had finally started to take off again.

And even though "'Mon Back" is an expression I've never heard before or since from anyone, I've used it in my consulting and everyone loves it.

THE STATUE OF LIBERTY SYNDROME

Jack was one of the most extraordinary entrepreneurs I have ever met. He literally started a business in his garage that he later sold to an international conglomerate for a net profit after taxes of tens of millions of US dollars. And this was before the internet made millionaires out of young people who just happened to be in the right place at the right time with a new idea.

Jack taught me how to fixed price my contracts. I was developing custom software for him and charging him on a time and materials basis. I thought I was doing everything right. I met with the people who would be using the programs and developed specifications that I had them review and then agree to. Sometimes I even developed a prototype so they could get the look and feel of how the software would work. Then I programmed, tested, and turned over the new software to them to test. Once everyone was satisfied I would move it into production.

I was working late one night and came up with some additional ideas and decided, rather than waiting until the next day, to add them to the programs. When I showed them the next day everyone was happy except Jack. He wanted to know what the new ideas would cost.

When I told him he said, "John, thanks for the free work. I'm not going to pay for it because we didn't agree it had to be done. Remember that no one spends my money except me. And, just to be sure that this doesn't happen again, from now on there won't be any more time and materials work; everything will be a fixed price."

So the next time Jack needed something I quoted him a price. But, it was before I had the detailed specifications. You can guess how much money I made on that. But because we had an agreement I went ahead and finished the work and only charged him what I had estimated.

And I really learned how to estimate and charge.

It was a turning point not only for my business but for my relationship with Jack.

"John," he said. "I always knew you were good technically, but I wasn't sure you knew how to run a business. You'll make a lot of money now, and, if you ever need any advice I'll be glad to help."

So I took him up on his offer. One of the things I remember was a discussion we had about hiring people. Jack had just let one of his vice-presidents go, even though the VP had increased the company's sales by 200%. I asked what happened.

"John, there were many reasons," Jack said. "I caught him with his secretary doing things in the office that belong in the bedroom. They were both married – not to each other – and I don't run that kind of an organization."

"We've learned a lot as we grew the organization. In the beginning we were more lax in our hiring and even more lax in our firing. We gave people too much leeway in their behavior.

In fact, we called it 'The Statue of Liberty Syndrome.' The Statue of Liberty has an encryption on the base that says, in part 'Give me your tired, your poor, your huddled masses yearning to breathe free.' It is a good testimonial to the freedom still found in the United States by immigrants. But, while it works well for the country, it is not necessarily a good foundation for a profit-making enterprise."

"John," Jack continued, "when we hire now we expect that their mothers have taught them how to dress, show up for work on time, and behave professionally. We put everyone on a ninety-day probation period, which corresponds with the laws of the state and the country, and the minute we find unacceptable behavior we let them go, regardless of how they perform their duties."

"Even though we have a good hiring process, there are still some people that have learned how to interview well so they get hired but don't work out. Keep this in mind as you grow your business. It will save you a lot of time and, even more important, a lot of money."

So, the next time you feel benevolent when you shouldn't, remember "The Statue of Liberty Syndrome".

It was in the mid 1970's and it was also the best time to sell your company if you were in the office machine distribution business. There were two international conglomerates vying aggressively with each other to be the biggest in the industry. So speed of acquisition rather than due diligence was the primary focus of the negotiators from the conglomerates, and it most often resulted in paying an inflated price, much to the delight of the entrepreneurs who owned the organizations they wanted to acquire.

The owners of the companies that were being acquired were different in many aspects, but they all had one thing in common: they were superb negotiators. It's how they built up their businesses from one-man operations to regional successes.

That's how Jack was able to make his millions. Not only was Jack a superb negotiator, he also had an unbelievable sense of foresight and timing.

He flew to New York with Vern, his Executive Vice-President, who was actually more of a Chief Operating Officer. Vern was previously the controller at the Mercedes dealership where Jack would take his cars for service. When Jack got behind on his payments -- he always paid as late as he could get away with – Vern would call and demand the money. And when the demands didn't work Vern wouldn't release the car the next time Jack brought it in for service until the back amounts were paid. This has become a standard practice in dealerships in the US but Vern was one of the pioneers in the idea.

Rather than anger him, it was Vern's tough stance on money that earned Jack's respect. So much so that when Jack was expanding and needed a controller he wouldn't stop until he convinced Vern that he had a better future with Jack than with the third-generation family Mercedes dealership.

So there they were, Jack and Vern, in New York having dinner at the Four Seasons with the Presidents of the two conglomerates on succeeding nights, with all expenses paid including first class airfare from Southern California to New York City.

You can guess who won the negotiations. Jack and Vern made a tentative deal with each of the conglomerates, flew back to Southern California, and then told each conglomerate the deal couldn't go through because they'd received a better offer.

It took a month before the negotiations were complete and Jack had doubled the selling price of his business, and included lucrative consulting contracts for him and Vern for the next five years.

And Jack's organization was just one of several who made similar deals. Every deal started over dinner and each one for more than the original offering price.

You can no doubt guess what followed. When the team from the conglomerate came in to fold the purchased organization into the conglomerate they uncovered some interesting things, all which would normally have been uncovered before an offer was made.

Hence the term "The Dinner Test" was added to the finance vocabulary of the conglomerate as an explanation of how they got into the mess. And when I find that my consulting clients have gotten themselves into messes I explain that they are using "The Dinner Test" approach to their negotiations.

After an explanation of what that means they all agree I was right, and they also agree to adopt a better method of negotiations in the future.

And before I take on a new client, I always try to schedule a dinner beforehand, so I have something to reference later.

I Could Sure Use Your Help

These are really magic words at any time, but especially when they come from a friend. It was back in the earlier days in my career, when I was still primarily technical, but moving into project management. My good friend Eric was close to the end of his career. However, instead of sitting back and relaxing, he had taken on a huge software development effort. And he knew enough to know how much trouble he was in.

We first met when Eric was a manager of computer software applications for a company that processed employee benefit information for union trust funds.

The company had decided to move from mainframe computers to the smaller mid-range computers that were just coming onto the market, and they were completely re-engineering all of their applications at the same time. It turned out to be a very ambitious undertaking that required the influx of a number of programmers more familiar with the new computers. And that's how Eric and I had the opportunity to get to know each other.

It was exciting work and I was good at it, and able to bring the project to completion ahead of schedule. Eric tried to hire me but I had picked up another contract and told him to stay in touch.

Over the next eighteen months we talked with each other off and on and I learned of his new position -- Data Processing Manager of a small union trust fund. I was just about to begin a new contract when Eric called again.

"John," he said, "remember when you said to call you if I ever needed help? Well, this is the call.

Things were going so well for me here I decided to re-write one of our major systems. And it seemed to be going along well -- until we tried to run some tests -- and, to make a long story short, I'm in real trouble. I could sure use your help."

I told Eric I was about to start a new contract and he asked if I could just come and look at what was happening and give him some advice. Now, how can you turn down an invitation like that from a friend? He even offered to pay me for my time and expenses.

So I drove the 100+ miles (160+ kilometers) from San Diego California USA to Los Angeles California USA to take a look at what was happening.

And I found out that my friend was indeed in trouble in more ways than one. The project manager had contracted a strange virus in the middle of the project (see the next story for more on this). One of the programmers decided he was infatuated with one of the young women using the computer and was sending her some rather explicit messages. The messages were all well-received until the programmer and the young woman had a falling-out and now it was a huge management issue for Eric. Another programmer was always a few minutes late because she was recently separated from her husband and had to drop her daughter off at school. She was about to be fired because she was late too many times. And, to make things even more interesting, Eric's son, who had previously been a very level-headed young man, and was helping in the department, became a typical teenager and decided to dye his hair orange and wear a t-shirt with a non-union slogan on it on the same day the board of directors had a meeting and wanted to see the computer department.

Now, how in the world could I possibly turn down this golden opportunity? So I told my other client they would have to wait, rented an apartment so I wouldn't have to commute every day, and began what would turn out to be a several year engagement that would change my life.

And all of this happened because a friend knew how to ask for help.

When I first met her, Nettie always had a frown on her face. Part of the reason was habit, and part of it was because she was recovering from Epstein Barr virus. It's not a common disease so you probably haven't heard about it. But you don't want to get it. It saps your energy and affects your thinking, and it's difficult to diagnose.

Nettie was the project manager I mentioned in a previous story that was working for my friend Eric. She had single-handedly rewritten a complicated medical and dental claims processing system that saved the organization a great deal of money. After a brief rest from that endeavor, she was asked if she could tackle their decades-old contribution accounting system.

For those of you who aren't familiar with employee benefit trust funds for unions in the US, you probably don't realize how complicated their contribution accounting is. Union employers contribute to a variety of funds for their union workers based upon the hours they work and their classification (journeyman, apprentice, etc.). The funds vary but can include pension, 401(k), health and welfare (medical), vacation and holiday, and others. And the rules that govern the amount of money allocated to each fund change based upon board meetings that are held periodically.

When Eric's contribution accounting system was originally developed, it was based upon some simple and very straightforward rules. Over the years the rules had changed, getting more and more complex along the way, and the old system had been modified to the point that it was difficult to make any more changes.

Nettie had outlined the improvements that needed to be made and put the people to work on the pieces, saving the more difficult ones for herself. Things were progressing according to plan when the Epstein Barr virus hit. At first, she just thought she had worn herself out and needed a rest. But as time went on she realized it was more than that.

But the doctor visits and the tests didn't reveal anything. And the contribution accounting system replacement project got further and further behind. It was in real trouble when my friend Eric called, asking for help.

Nettie, however, wasn't ready for the help. She knew something was wrong with her, but she didn't know what it was and wasn't ready to admit that she just couldn't stay in charge.

So I did what I usually do in tense situations; I ignored the silent and sometimes not so silent protests, dug into the complex programs, and waited. In less time than I anticipated, the programmers started to ask questions.

"What's this for? Why are we doing it this way? Have you thought about what will happen if ..."

And instead of answering the questions I said, "Let's talk about it." And I got with everyone including Nettie and sat back and listened.

After a while, Nettie would ask what I thought. As time went on, whenever someone would ask her what she thought, she'd say "Let's ask John."

As we began to move the project forward, I initiated standard project management techniques including periodic status meetings and management reporting.

And I helped my friend clean up the people issues. The programmer apologized to the young woman he had been flirting with and she stopped her complaints. The other programmer made up with her husband and started showing up on time. Eric convinced his son it was in both their best interest if he found another job before he was fired, so the son listened and soon left.

And Nettie and I went to lunch, declared a truce, and decided we would be co-project managers. Best of all, Nettie found a doctor who gave her a correct diagnosis and she was relieved to find out her disease wasn't just in her head, wasn't life-threatening, and with some rest would go away.

So she took some time off while we finished the project. But, before she did, she sat with my friend and admitted, in her own way, that she was glad to get the help.

"Sometimes our ego gets in the way. He's better than I am now, but not as good as I used to be," she said to resolve her conflicting emotions. My friend had the wisdom to agree with her and so did I, and that made it work for all of us.

Working with entrepreneurs can be rewarding, and also an exceptional learning experience, as you could see from my story about Jack. But it has its quirks. Just ask my client and friend Roger.

Roger was the Vice President of Finance for a small entrepreneurial organization. But he claimed that was only his hobby; his real occupation was a pilot. Roger was more than a pilot; he was a humanitarian pilot. Roger was a member of an organization that would fly doctors from San Diego, California in the US to small towns in Mexico to treat people for free. The organization consisted of people who thought that children shouldn't be denied proper healthcare just because they had the bad luck to be born on the wrong side of the border between the US and Mexico.

The business side of Roger was as good as the humanitarian side; he refused to tolerate anything but first-class performance, and rewarded people for it. I met Roger because I was referred to him when he needed some management consulting. His small entrepreneurial company had just taken over a much larger company -- and he had inherited an Information Technology department that was sorely in need of repair.

The sales and marketing people had ganged up against the manufacturing people, claiming they couldn't make enough of what could be sold, and the solution they came up with was to purchase and implement a new complicated sales forecasting system for the computer on an impossible schedule. So the sales and marketing people had managed to rope in the IT department as well. That is, until Roger showed up and began to question everything.

The IT department fell under Roger's finance arm. That placement of IT was quite common at the time, and in this case it was the right place to have it. Roger told me that while the problem was presented to him as the lack of the IT department's ability to respond, he suspected there was more to the story and wanted to know what to do. He said he'd learned over the years that things aren't always what they might seem at first.

After interviewing everyone involved, it became obvious that one of the real problems was the ability of the sales and marketing people to forecast, regardless of the software available to assist with the process. And this was compounded by the decision everyone had made to build product to forecast rather than based upon sales, which meant the new software, when it finally worked, was going to make the problem worse rather than better.

The acting IT manager had aligned himself with the sales and marketing department, and was cracking the whip on the IT people, who were all looking for a job anywhere else that was sane, rather than put up with the craziness. It was an interesting interview with the IT manager because he proved to be so insensitive he thought I was there to confirm that he should be offered the job permanently.

To make matters even more complicated, the company that had installed the computer system in the small entrepreneurial company that Roger came from was trying to convince him they had the perfect solution for the new organization.

No wonder Roger wanted an expert and unbiased opinion about what to do.

After we felt we had the real and complete story about what was happening, we decided to solve the problem one piece at a time. We told the company that had installed the computer system in Roger's previous company that, while we were most appreciative for what they had been able to do before, their solution just wouldn't work in the new company.

We told the acting IT Manager it was time for him to find a new job. And we told him he could start looking immediately because he didn't need to come to work for us anymore.

We promoted the manager in charge of computer operations to become the new IT Manager because when we interviewed him he had the right attitude and obvious managerial skills.

We purchased some productivity and reporting software and hired a recent college graduate and trained her how to use it to satisfy day to day ad hoc reporting capability.

We slowed down the effort to install the new software to a more reasonable schedule, and told the sales and marketing people to improve their ability to forecast, using the reports our recent college graduate was able to provide.

Throughout the process, we worked closely together to make certain our thoughts were synchronized. I had never worked for a company that had been able to buy out a larger company; I thought that was something that only happened in the movies.

So one day I asked Roger how they had been able to put the deal together.

"John," he said, "I had nothing to do with it. It was all George's doing." George was the entrepreneur that had started the first company and been able to get it to the point that he had enough equity built up to be able to put the deal together to buy out the larger one.

"George is an absolute genius when it comes to putting deals together. But managing the results; that's a different story. I guess that's why he hired me and it's the same reason I hired you. You have to know when you need to get help for the things you don't know how to do."

"Let me tell you one of my favorite stories about George and you'll understand. In the middle of putting the deal together for this company, George walked through the office of the old company one day and saw a man sitting back in his chair with his feet up on his desk. George turned more shades of red than a Picasso, stormed into my office, and told me to fire the man. I asked him who he meant."

"He said to follow him and I'd see. So I went with him and, when I saw who he was referring to, I turned to him and said 'George, that's our Chief Scientist. He's the one who's responsible for all of our patents.'"

"George blinked, immediately calmed down, and said 'Roger, what's wrong with you? Why didn't you say so earlier? Give him a raise.'"

I have some other stories about entrepreneurs, but "Give Him a Raise" is still one of my favorites. And it's a good lesson for all of us about how sometimes things aren't what they might seem at first.

After a few years, my client and friend Roger had moved on to another organization. We kept in touch by telephone off and on over the years but it had been some time since I saw him.

Roger called, told me he had moved on to another company, and wanted to see me. I went to his new company, and Roger gave me a tour. He then explained his problems, and, in his forthright manner, told me, "John I need your help, but I'm too new here to ask the President for the money to pay you".

Based upon our past relationship, and the current state of my business which was very profitable, I told him it was all right, I would still help but would give him an invoice later when he could justify it.

The company, like the last one Roger worked for, was another entrepreneurial organization and they were interesting; they manufactured products that turned salt water into fresh water. Even though the process and manufacturing were crude they were beginning to make significant progress towards streamlining their operations and had begun to make a profit.

But they had problems with their Information Technology department. Roger hadn't been there very long before he started hearing a number of complaints about the IT Manager, Jim. Not surprisingly, Jim had similar complaints about other people in the company.

Trying to make sense out of the conflicting stories, I used the same approach I use everywhere when there is confusion about the truth; I interviewed everyone involved. As both Roger and I suspected, the problem was with the IT manager. The stories of verbal abuse I heard from everyone in the organization were unbelievable.

So I gathered up the findings and reported to Roger. Roger was the type of executive who wanted to hear what you had discovered before it was written in a formal report, so I summarized my interviews and conclusions.

Roger thought for a minute, and then said "So what you're telling me, John, is that anyone in my organization should be able to go to Jim and talk. Except for making certain Jim isn't busy, they shouldn't have to make an appointment, or prepare a formal request. They should be received courteously, tell Jim what they need in layman's terms, receive a reasonable response, and be advised when they can expect an estimate of effort and a schedule for completion."

"Now, what's so hard about that?"

It's a nice line that I've used on multiple occasions when counseling people about their behavior. Feel free to steal it.

Armed with detailed examples, but believing in second and even third chances for people, Roger sat down with Jim and told him what he found out and what he expected from Jim to make things right. And to Jim's credit, even though he was taken by surprise, he listened and appeared to change.

So everything was fine for a while, until in a company meeting one morning Jim blurted out an unbelievably inappropriate comment to a female manager that I won't try to clean up for this story. That was enough for Roger. He was ready to fire Jim. But I asked Roger if he had entered anything in Jim's personnel file and he admitted he hadn't because he wanted to give Jim a chance first to redeem himself. I warned Roger about the laws in affect at the time in the state and had him check with the Human Resources Department Manager. It turned out my warning was correct and before we could fire Jim we had to get him some counseling.

So we put Jim into counseling and I sat down with him for a talk. I suggested that if he wanted to further his career it might best be done somewhere else. The employment market was good at the time and Jim took the advice and moved on to a more technical position where he didn't have to manage anyone but himself.

We promoted one of the people under Jim to IT manager. He had a more reasonable approach to human relations, and everyone in the organization breathed a sigh of relief and went back to business.

Now, what's so hard about that?

Don't Stop to Admire Your Serve

There are undoubtedly some of you who have personally experienced the problems of being a road warrior where you on a plane every Sunday or Monday and not back home until Friday or Saturday. The rest of you, I am certain, can imagine what it is like. It has its advantages; the frequent flier miles come in handy when you want to take a vacation. But it can be a lonely existence so you work out ways to cope with it.

I did some traveling in the early 1990's when I left every week from Southern California in the US to go to Vancouver, Canada for a consulting engagement. But my real business traveling didn't start until the late 1990's, when I decided to look for a very large Year 2000 Readiness (Y2K) contract. You probably remember those days -- either by personal experience or reading about them -- where all kinds of disasters were predicted that never came to fruition.

I looked at a number of possible engagements, ultimately rejecting most of them for a variety of reasons, including they weren't large enough, long enough, or complicated enough for what I was trying to accomplish. The contract I ultimately selected was for the Goodyear Tire and Rubber Company and was based in Akron Ohio in the US – almost a continent away from Southern California where I lived at the time. The engagement was run by IBM and was certainly large enough; it involved all of the North American plants (US and Canada) and executive consulting for their other plants worldwide. It was an exciting time, but also a long engagement – it lasted 27 months – and the weekly traveling got old.

My wife is an artist, and even though she had her studio at home, could sketch and paint anywhere. Our children were already adults by then, so she was able to break the monotony of my traveling and instead come join me sometimes. She is also an avid tennis player who had been after me for years to learn, so I decided to surprise her and fill some of my spare time with tennis lessons. I found a tennis club not far from where I was staying and signed up for a series of lessons. And for those of you familiar with the geography, I was lucky enough to find an indoor club, where I could still go during the long winters.

It took more than one series of lessons – I've never been a natural athlete – but I was very fortunate to find a wonderful instructor. Beth was the head professional at the club and had infinite patience; a trait that came in extremely handy when she gave me lessons. She was expecting her first child and it was a joy to watch as she still somehow managed to look graceful on the court even as the child within her grew.

I grasped the basic concepts fairly soon, and was able to return the forehands and eventually the backhands with a measure of consistency. But learning to serve was another story. And even if you don't play tennis, you have probably watched enough professional tennis on television to have an appreciation for the important part the serve plays in the game.

For those of you who don't play tennis, what makes the serve so complicated is the coordination of both hands, the importance of the correct ball toss, the coiling of the body ... well I'm sure you get the idea; it's not an easy thing to do.

I must have had at least a dozen lessons before I started to grasp the concept, and was able to get the ball in the court where it was supposed to be. After great deal of practice, I found I could even begin to place the ball close to where I wanted it to.

Beth had a drill where I would serve the ball and she would return it, requiring sometimes a backhand and sometimes a forehand return. Eventually I got to where she could surprise me with her return and I could still get it back.

I was feeling pretty good one session and hit what I thought was a wonderful serve that went right into the corner where I had aimed it and skidded along the court. I couldn't believe it and stood there and gazed with wonder at what I had done. It looked good, that is, until she flicked her racket for an easy return and caught me flat-footed.

Beth smiled and said, "Next time, don't stop to admire your serve."

How often, in the normal course of events in our day, do we find ourselves stopping when we should continue and finish what we started and keep ourselves prepared for what is coming next? There's always time later to reflect on our accomplishments; if we do it at the wrong time it gets in the way of reaching our goal.

In the course of my career I have quite often found myself mentoring some of my clients to help them accomplish more. And, of all the stories I relate in the mentoring, Beth's advice is the one that everyone tells me stays with them.

THEY WERE PATIENT WITH THEIR LIVES

During the fall of the year the turning of the tree leaves in parts of the US is a magnificent event. There is a train that goes though the Cuyahoga Valley in Ohio where you can view the multi-colored foliage up close. It's a spectacular sight, and it's worth finding a similar landscape in your corner of the world, even if you're not an artist.

As you can imagine, my wife found the subject fascinating and produced some very memorable paintings. But in the process she said "It would be nice to find someone from here that I could learn from so I can capture this feeling like a native would."

Fortunately, I was able to find a local seminar taught by Don Andrews, a former student of Robert E. Wood, who was my wife's original and always favorite instructor. Over the years Don had become a famous watercolorist in his own right, out of the shadow of his mentor, and he gave seminars all over the world. Don said one of the reasons he chose Akron was because of the spectacular landscape, especially in the fall.

The seminar consisted of a combination of classes in a studio and field trips to various locations. It was very well attended, and we were extremely lucky to get into the class, only because of a last-minute cancellation. My wife was the only person who traveled across the country to attend; everyone else was local.

The work of everyone was impressive. Most of the people were accomplished artists who had been painting for years. And there was a camaraderie that only comes from people in the same profession, passionate about what they do and working together intensely for a few days.

Whatever your profession, I hope you have experienced that feeling in workshops and seminars that you have attended in your area of expertise. If not, you are attending the wrong ones, and need to look for something else.

In addition to the time in the classes and field trips, there was time as well to get to know each other by simply being together and sharing stories.

Most of the people in her class had been born in or near Akron. They had grown up there, some attending the same school, had met and married local people, and settled down and raised their families there.

It was the same in some ways, but very different in others, from the experiences of my wife, who was born in Cotabato, a small city in the province of Mindanao in the Philippines. She moved several times when she was young and ultimately was courted by a man from the large metropolitan city of Manila, the heart of which, Makati, is very similar to Manhattan in New York City in the US.

They married and settled in Manila, requiring the adjustment of anyone who moves from a very rural setting to a large city. She worked in the guidance office of Ateneo de Manila, one of the most prestigious schools in Asia. She and her two sons would wake before dawn to take the bus together for hours to get to school. For years, until the politics and her personal situation changed, her life was, therefore, in many ways, similar to the lives of the people in Akron.

But things change. To be able to support her family she went to work for a cousin who owned a media business.

This worked well for her until the early 1980's when the media business evaporated after Ferdinand Marcos, the dictator who had declared martial law and taken over the country, was overthrown in the "People Power" revolution.

She was struggling to feed her family, and give them a future, when she learned that, through a strange quirk of timing, she could claim her American citizenship. Her grandfather was an

American citizen, and she was born in a small window of time where that lineage was enough for her to claim her citizenship.

The effort was daunting. Her birth records had been destroyed when the hospital where she was born burned during the war. Other pertinent records had been destroyed as well. And, as often happens when dealing with governments, she received inconsistent and often conflicting requirements about what she needed to claim her citizenship, depending upon whom she talked to in the American Consulate.

But, one thing was clear: to make the citizenship happen, she would have to be in America. So, she sold her only possession – her house – for a pittance which gave her just enough money for her plane fare to the United States.

She arrived in San Francisco, California in the US and stayed with friends. She got a job working in a gas station at night so she could spend the days pursuing her citizenship. The gas station was in a less than desirable neighborhood, and she was fortunate to be in a locked booth.

During the day she went to the American Consulate, where she would talk with different people, each giving somewhat conflicting advice, until someone finally told her the best thing she could do was to talk to Senator Cranston.

So early one morning she went to his office, where she was told by his gatekeeper he was too busy to see her. But, by then she had had enough of people pushing her away, and sat outside the Senator's office all day long. No lunch, no bathroom breaks, no water, she just waited. Until after eight o'clock in the evening when the Senator finally came out of the office. He did a double-take and said "Who are you?"

She said "I've been waiting here since seven this morning and people tell me you are the only one who can help me."

These were the magic words. The senator brought her into his office, listened to her story, and gave her a list of what she needed to do.

It wasn't easy. Because of the burned records, the list of tasks included hours of research in the library, painstakingly going through microfilmed records, to find an article about her grandfather. He was, in his own way, famous. He was a pharmacist who had opened what he called the American Pharmacy in the remote town of Zamboanga City in the province of Mindanao in the Philippines. His pharmacy looked like one of the vintage pharmacies in America, including a soda fountain.

Everyone in the area knew about the American Pharmacy; it was the local gathering place.   And her grandfather was doing extremely well until, one day, two men in the pharmacy started arguing about what one of them was doing to the other's wife and they challenged each other to a duel. Only the duel started right then and there in the pharmacy, where one of the men drew a pistol, pointed it at the other, and shot. In an effort to save the other man, the grandfather moved in front of him and caught the bullet and was killed.

It was a big story. Enough that it went beyond the local papers and my wife was able to find it, decades later, by using the Soundex machine in San Francisco, California in the US, continents away.

It turned out to be a crucial piece of the documentation that was needed, and my wife ultimately became an American citizen.

By the time I met her she was an apartment manager in Los Angeles, California, living with one of her sons. The other son was recently married and living in the same building. When she became an American citizen, she had been able to petition her sons and fly them to America so they could be together.

A few years later, after we were married, we had the pleasure of attending the ceremony where the married son claimed his

American Citizenship. My wife's dream had been finally realized; she had given her sons the opportunity she believed they needed and were entitled to.

My goodness, what a different life my wife had from everyone else in the class.

But when I asked her about the differences, she thought for a moment and said, simply, "They were patient with their lives."

What got us to where we are in life won't necessarily move us forward to where we want to be. It's important to know the pace we have maintained to be able to set the pace for the future.

If you haven't been moving fast enough, it's probably time to speed up. But if you've been in too much of a hurry, perhaps it's time to be more patient with your life.

I got the call on a Friday night. We were celebrating the birthday of a friend and our house was full of people. The noise from the party was so loud I could hardly hear the caller.

"John," the caller, who also happened to be named John said, "remember that deal I told you about last year with General Motors?"

"Yes," I replied, "the one we both got all excited about and then nothing happened.
I remember it well. I rearranged some other business waiting for General Motors to come through and then the deal died."

"Well," John said, "it's been resurrected. General Motors changed their main supplier to Lockheed Martin. They told Lockheed to reserve their good people and then they ended up negotiating for months before they finally closed the deal. Lockheed lost patience when their senior people had been sitting on the bench longer than they expected with no incoming revenue to offset their high salaries and put them back to work right before the contract finally came through. Now they need people."

"Sounds good," I said. "When do we start?"

"Well," John said, "how about next Tuesday?"

"Have them send me a plane ticket and I'll rearrange my schedule," I replied. "This is too good to pass up."

As it worked out it took another week before the plane ticket came through. And that was just as well because I was still living in Southern California in the US and the contract was for over a year in Singapore and I had a lot to do to get ready to be away for that long.

I flew into Detroit, Michigan in the US and we started to prepare. It was a contract to mentor the organization's project managers on their new methodology they used to manage their Information Technology projects. The first portion of the contract consisted of presentations by the customer's personnel about General Motors' methodology for managing IT projects so we would be able to train their people all over the world.

I was to run the Asian portion of the engagement and brought in Delores from Melbourne, Australia and Rick from Hong Kong to help. There were other people already in place in Europe and North America with plans for Mexico and South America.

When we checked with the customer's Singapore people, they admitted they weren't ready for us yet. We also learned that all they did in Singapore was to get on an airplane to fly somewhere else in Asia. The company had commissioned a study and determined that Singapore was central in Asia and the air fares were the cheapest from there so that's where they put their Asian headquarters.

We were staffed for Australia and China, but what they really needed help with was a large project in Tokyo, Japan.

I had previously done business with a number of Japanese-based businesses and knew there would be no way to mentor them in Tokyo unless you spoke Japanese. Unfortunately my ability to speak different languages is worse than my ability to learn sports and if you've been reading these stories in order you already have an idea of what that means.

So we started a search for an expert in Information Technology that also spoke Japanese and got lucky. We found Puja, a wonderful lady from India with a PhD who was in Tokyo working for another company. Her contract with them was about to expire so she was looking for something else because she wanted to stay in Tokyo for a while.

In the early part of July I boarded a plane to Singapore to coordinate everything. In case you've never been there, take a look at a globe and you'll see that Singapore is right on the equator and it's not the place you want to be in July. But to get through the summer months they have a wonderful series of underground tunnels complete with shops and restaurants, all fully air conditioned. You'll find the same thing in Houston, Texas in the US and it really works until you have to go outside and then you remember why you want to stay in the tunnels.

I met all the people and they were aloof at first, but when they found out I was really there to help and not a spy from headquarters to report on all of their shortcomings, we got along fine. I showed up in a suit and tie and they said this wasn't allowed in Singapore in the summer so we held a formal ceremony to cut off my tie and tack it to the wall along with the ties of every other person who had shown up from Detroit.

We flew together to Tokyo and started looking at the project. The organization had bought out a smaller company and wanted to replace their custom-built software with something more modern so they were looking at a number of packages on the market.

And as different people found out this project had money they kept trying to add their requirements to it. The company made vehicles so the best analogy I can offer is the project started out to make a bicycle and ended up with something that was a combination of a bicycle, motorcycle, automobile, truck and bus.

We sat around trying to make some sense out of this when Puja, the lady with the PhD, said, "It's what's 'not' included that I'm worried about. How are we going to explain this so it's clear to everyone?"

That's all it took. We drew a diagram showing what the project was trying to accomplish, surrounded by all the things that the project 'wouldn't' do. We then met with everyone separately who was trying to hang things onto the project and explained if they could find the money and get their project approved we'd be glad to tackle it for them.

With Asia taken care of I returned to Detroit and got to spend time there with senior executives and project managers in every area of their business. The only problem was I ended up in Singapore in the heart of the summer and Detroit in the heart of the winter.

I guess nothing's perfect.

It was a few years after the turn of the century and I was consulting for the finance division of an automotive manufacturer. I had been there for some time and was well liked and respected. In fact, I was so well liked and respected, that when they got in trouble with a critical project, they wanted to tell the project manager they no longer needed his services, and put me in charge.

I still had quite a few active projects that, while they were winding down, still required quite a bit of attention, and needed to be completed, so I made the organization a deal: I would take over their troubled project if they would find someone to finish my projects.

There was a wonderful fellow already working for them who was commuting from the Eastern part of the US to Southern California in the Southwest portion of the country. Bruce was waiting for some new projects to begin and had the time available and was willing to complete my old ones.

It sounded like a perfect solution. And it was, until circumstances got in the way. It took much longer than expected to find the right person to take over the troubled project, and Bruce found another job.

It wasn't Bruce's fault. The deal he had made with his company was they would find someone local to Southern California to take over for him while they found him some work near his home town. After two years they said they were still looking, so Bruce did some looking on his own. His search was successful. He found a job with better pay a few miles from his house.

Bruce apologized for leaving, and was very sincere, but the truth is, it was time for him to go home. He had done more than his part to make certain his company was represented well, and he did an exemplary job to make certain the client's projects were executed well. Overshadowing the work was the fact that he had a sixteen year old daughter at home who had just passed her driving test, and a recently widowed mother who was all alone, so he needed to be there for them.

So I ended up with the new troubled project along with all of my old ones that hadn't finished, and also had some new ones lurking in the wings that needed to start right away. Needless to say, I wasn't sitting around bored and looking for something to do. Just finishing the weekly status reports took up the most part of two full days.

Every day I would come in early, and before checking my email for the several hundred messages that would be there, I would take a few deep breaths, take off my jacket, and say to no one in particular "New Day." It was a reminder that each day brings not only challenges, but also the opportunity to solve some of the problems and make some progress.

Time solved the dilemma; we finally found someone to take over the troubled project, some of the other projects ended, and life got bearable again.

But, one of the people that I sat close to came up to me and said, "John, you know what I'll remember the most about you?"

I was almost afraid to hear the answer, but said "No, tell me. And why is it you're talking about remembering me? I don't recall telling you I am going anywhere."

"I'll remember how every day you would come in and say 'New Day' no matter what you had faced the day before or thought you were going to face that day. I've had some troubled times in my life recently, and it was a reminder that we get to start over each day. Without that reminder I'm not sure what I would have done. And it took several weeks before I understood."

"I haven't been very happy here, and it gave me the impetus to look for a new job. I just got an offer that I accepted, and of all the things I'll bring that with me from working here with you, it's the one that's most important. And, I promise to do the same thing each day, so someone else can hopefully learn the same lesson."

I hope the lesson works for you. Pass it on.

WHAT KEEPS YOU UP AT NIGHT?

There are a lot of articles, books and lectures about stress. No, not how to get stressed; it turns out we are all pretty good at that part. Most are more about how to deal with stress once it's there.

The tension relievers include how to breathe right, what to eat, what not to eat, how to prepare your mind for what might come in life, and a number of other techniques, ranging from the useful to the bizarre.

What you don't read much about is the stress that helps us. For example, while it is stressful for almost every entertainer right before they go on stage, it turns out the great ones will tell you it helps them give a good performance.

And there are quite a few funny movies about what happens to everyone before and during a wedding.

Since my consulting evolved into mostly million US dollar Information Technology projects, many of them already in trouble when I was asked to intercede, I'm not a stranger to stress.

It's where I learned the benefits – not the negative aspects – of stress. I was staffing for a large, mission-critical project. I had hired several project managers, and most of the lead personnel including a technical lead, a testing lead, a communications lead, and some others. We had gone through some standard techniques to learn to work together better as a team and begun to formulate our plans.

We were reviewing the plans with one of the senior managers and were proud of what we had done. The plans were well received, and we thought we were well prepared. He had asked us several questions, and we had answers that we thought were excellent to every one of the questions.

We had the answers, that is, until he leaned back, smiled, and said "Well, this all sounds pretty good. I've only got one more question. What keeps you up at night?"

The room got silent. It was a question we had never anticipated. We thought about it for a while, and then each of the managers that I had hired came up with something that none of us had thought about before.

We were able to come up with the answers to what we needed to do with each anticipated problem, but that process took several hours. And this was after we all believed we had thought of everything. Having the answers helped relieve the stress, but the process itself was quite stressful. Much of life is that way; stress relief is often more about preparedness than about attitude.

I also learned a very valuable lesson about one of the important differences between managers and senior managers – the ability to ask the right question at the right time.

So, what keeps you up at night?

YOU'RE TRYING TO PUT YOUR CHILDREN THROUGH COLLEGE; I'M TRYING TO FEED THEM

He was the President of the American division of a major worldwide automotive manufacturing company. And he had the unfortunate luck to be promoted on the eve of the worst recession in the United States since the Great Depression in the 1920's, and also the worst recession in automotive history in the United States. It brought many American companies into bankruptcy, led to the replacement of the long-time president of the American icon General Motors, and caused an Asian-based automotive company to post the first quarterly loss in its history.

Earlier in the year we had finally done something people had been trying to do for years; we obtained approval to proceed with a multi-million-US Dollar Information Technology project to replace a decades-old system that handled automotive warranty.

And we had started to hire people, to build a foundation for the replacement system.

When the recession hit, the organization did the smart thing; they stopped all of their major Information Technology projects. And since we were the largest project, we were at the top of the list to stop.

Disappointed, but undaunted, we tried to see if we could slow down the project instead of stop it. We re-evaluated our staffing, and reduced the current fiscal year expenditure to a small percentage of what we had originally forecast.

After a great deal of preparation, including a thorough analysis and what we thought was a very persuasive presentation, we went in front of the President.

He listened politely and told us no, we couldn't slow down the project; he was still stopping it. However, realizing how much this meant to us, he explained further.

"You must understand," he said, "I am in a very difficult position. We are facing a terrible recession; it's the worse for our industry that I have ever lived through. And I have stopped investment not only in Information Technology, but also across the board in capital improvements. And I'm not canceling your project; I'm just putting it on hold. Do you have children," he inquired? We all said yes, we did. "How old are they" he asked?

Among us they were various ages, ranging from newborn through grade school and high school, with some in college and some graduated with families and children of their own. He asked if we did things to take care of them – basic things like sending them to school and clothing and feeding them. "Of course," we all replied.

"Well, then, let me put it this way" he said. "You're trying to put your children through college; I'm trying to feed them."

There's not much you can say to that argument. So we went away and came back a year later, when the economy was better, and received permission to start the project again. Timing is sometimes everything.

We're Running Out of Time; We'd Better Slow Down

As you may have gathered by now, sports are not my forte. But I'm not completely clueless about how sports are played; I'm just not very good at playing them. This means I know that the title of this story doesn't apply to running a race or playing a football or basketball or baseball game.

But there are times when it does apply, especially in business, and especially in multi-million US dollar Information Technology projects, which are my specialty. I take over a great deal of extremely troubled projects, and find that often one of the problems is they have been moving too fast.

Projects all have deadlines. We call them milestones and they represent significant events that demonstrate progress. Each milestone has a specific deliverable along with a deadline for its completion.

We all know about deadlines even if we didn't know what they are called. They exist everywhere in our lives and start as children when our mothers tell us we need to be home at a specific time. And also universal is that sinking feeling that comes in the pit of our stomach as the deadline gets closer and there is still a lot of work to be done. This is the time we realize that without some kind of miracle, we just aren't going to make it.

There are only a few things we can do right to still meet the deadline, and a lot of things that we can do wrong.

One of the oldest techniques is to back off on what we had hoped to accomplish. But this just means, most of the time, postponing work that will still need to be done.

Another approach is to throw more people at the problem. Depending upon what you're trying to accomplish, this sometimes works.

But, often, especially when we are trying to accomplish complicated things, this leads to a lot of unnecessary expense and, still, a missed deadline.

How about just working longer hours? Like a sprint at the end of a long race. This, too, often works. In fact, it's the approach most often employed by people because it's so obvious. Indeed, sometimes it's the right thing to do and it works. When you ask people their contingency plan for when things go wrong it's often based upon this tactic.

But when you have a large team of people, already overwrought, and you try to push them even more to make a deadline, it can just confuse things. They not only don't get the work done; they make more mistakes along the way and, in addition to missing the deadline, they often produce a shoddy result.

Sometimes the best approach is to refocus everyone. It's the time to slow everyone down instead of speeding them up, and get them to think about what they are trying to do, and how to best get it done more efficiently.

Just tell them, "We're running out of time; we'd better slow down."

Since my wife and I were getting on in years (that's a euphemism for getting old, in case you haven't heard the expression) we decided we'd better find something besides tennis to keep us occupied and fit when we retired.

We liked to watch golf on television, and decided we would try our hand at it. We had no idea what we were in for. For those of you who play, our hats are off to you. And for those of you who don't, and would like a lesson in humility, I suggest you try it.

For something that looks simple when the professionals do it on television, it is an unbelievably complicated sport.

We tried first to get some books and hit some balls at the driving range. And while the books we found worked for us later, they were too complicated to help much at the beginning.

So we decided to go to a place where they sold golf clubs and see what we could pick up there. We were lucky enough to go the same day the owner, Roger, a former golf professional, was there. He watched us hit a few balls with one of the clubs and said, in his mild-mannered way "I think I can help you."

As you might imagine, there's never been more of an understatement. If anyone needed help it was us.

Roger started us with the basics: how to grip the club, how to line up the ball, where to place your feet, and how to swing. Fortunately Roger was a very patient man. And, my wife is a natural athlete, so she started to catch on much earlier than I did, which meant Roger could save his patience for me.

Roger first let me watch how he hit the ball. Then he put me in front of a mirror so I could see how it looked in comparison when I got set up and swung the club. It took a while before my swing began to even remotely resemble the way Roger's looked.

Then I tried to hit a ball. We were at a driving range near Hollywood, California in the US so, fortunately, people were more distracted by the celebrities that practiced there than my bad attempts at hitting a golf ball.

Until I got a little better it was dangerous to be too close to me because when I tried to hit the ball straight it would sometimes go at almost right angles. I'm not sure who needed more patience, Roger, my wife, or me.

I was so bad that when I started my lesson with Roger my wife found somewhere else to be, as far away from us as she could go. But nothing fazed Roger. He would sit on a stool in front of me -- he was approaching ninety years old and, while still very spry and capable, needed to sit while he placed balls on the practice tee, one after another, for me to hit.

And when my frustration would begin to rise, Roger would look at me, smile, and say "John, this is a very difficult game. But, eventually you'll start to catch on. Until you do, just hit another ball. And keep doing that until, finally, things will start to work out."

It has taken an extremely long time – think in terms of years instead of months. But even though I'm not ready to enter any tournaments, and rarely keep score, I can now play well enough to walk the course a few times a week with my wife and enjoy the exercise. And every once in a while I'll get lucky and hit the ball well and, sometimes, even make a par on an easy hole.

But every time I make a particularly bad shot I remember Roger. And I remember his advice: "Just hit another ball." It keeps the blood pressure down and makes the game enjoyable, even when I don't do well.

The advice, of course, works for most everything in life. Try it the next time you find yourself in a difficult and frustrating spot. It helps more than you might think.

The Ball Has No Memory

Our friend Charles gets credit for this saying. But, if you happen to be a gambler, you might recognize the phrase "The Dice Have No Memory" which communicates the same mathematical and management message.

Charles is our golf buddy. We play with him once or twice a week, which is plenty for us because we walk the course for the exercise instead of using a golf cart, even though the course is quite hilly, and the exercise tires us out.

Charles started out playing golf later in life and he had the world's strangest golf swing, but enough time has passed and he's had enough practice that he keeps up with us now and even sometimes beats us.

Besides, he's a really delightful fellow, and a real pleasure to be with on and off the golf course.

Every time Charles would hit a particularly bad shot, which is quite easy to do even if you've been playing for a while, he'd say "I sometimes forget the ball has no memory."

So we asked him one day why he said this and what it meant.

"It's simple," Charles said. "Every time I address the ball for another shot I have to remember that this time I have a very good chance of hitting it right instead of the lousy shot I had last time."

"If I didn't look at golf that way I probably would have given up long ago. But it's the trying that makes you better, not the mistakes you make when you try."

And it certainly started to work for Charles. After a seemingly endless number of tries, he started to get better. His golf swing looks almost professional now, and quite often he hits the ball straight and far. It's a real pleasure now to watch him play.

And let's not forget that the same mathematical and management message applies to almost everything we do. Just because we failed when we tried something the first few times doesn't mean we'll continue to fail.

In fact, odds are in our favor that, if we're trying to do something we're ultimately capable of, the more we keep trying, the more likely we are to succeed.

You see, it's not only the ball and the dice that have no memory, it's also our failures. Of course our own memories sometimes persist in keeping us from trying harder, but you can overcome that problem too.

SHE MUST HAVE BEEN BEAUTIFUL WHEN SHE WAS YOUNG

We were playing golf when we saw our caddies talking to the caddy of the player behind us.

And they were all smiling. I asked my wife to find out what was happening.

She talked with the caddies, smiled, and told me the doctor who was playing behind us paid her a compliment. I asked what it was, suspecting it had nothing to do with her golfing prowess.

She said he told the caddy "She must have been beautiful when she was young," referring, of course, to my wife.

I must admit the doctor couldn't have been more correct. Even though the decades have changed her dark hair to white, she still is the most beautiful woman I have ever seen.

But I thought it was a strange way to give someone a compliment.

"You still don't understand the Filipino culture, do you?" said my wife. "Believe it or not, I often hear that, and, if you think about it, it's really a polite way to tell someone how pretty they are."

"If you say so," I replied. But I still thought it was strange, and have used the story with our friends many times, much to the amusement of everyone.

Not long after that day we had a visit from a niece whom we hadn't seen for a long time. Her husband looked at all the pictures we have around the house, and commented to us about my wife, "My goodness, you were really beautiful when you were young."

So I thought about what my wife had said earlier, about not really understanding the Filipino culture, and decided she might be right. And I thought about the many times I had dealt with different cultures in my consulting, and decided there were times when I could have handled things better.

So the next time you're ready to interpret -- in the wrong way -- what someone from a different background says, remember, you just might not realize what they really mean.

No wonder we still make mistakes, especially in dealing with people, no matter how old and wise we think we are.

LIFE'S LESSONS ARE REPEATED UNTIL THEY'RE LEARNED

If you've read the other stories in this book about my wife, you've probably concluded that she's a remarkable woman.

You couldn't be more correct. And she gets credit once again for teaching me about life with the phrase "Life's lessons are repeated until they're learned."

She said she learned this from a friend whom she met when she was working with a group of psychologists at Ateneo University in Manila in the Philippines decades ago.

She said it to me one night after work when I complained about something stupid that I had just done that day. "I know better," I told her, "and I did it anyway."

Quite frankly, I don't even remember the mistake that I made. I make so many it's hard to remember which one triggered the comment.

But she said it in earnest, and, for some reason, it has stuck with me over the years.

So now, I try to remember the comment when I am facing a difficult situation, and know I'm about to do or say something stupid.

And, sometimes, the pause before I act or say anything even works. Rather than make the same mistake I've made so many times before, I come up with something different to do or say.

Unfortunately, I don't always come up with the right thing to do or say, but at least I can say I tried.

But, often, I do handle the situation better ... sometimes even better than I thought that I could ever do.

And I always remember her comment "Life's lessons are repeated until they're learned." And I smile and am glad again that I've learned when to take advice.

You Can't Learn How to Be Taller

One of the more rewarding but difficult things we do as managers and senior managers is place people in the right position. Hopefully, we also place them at the right time, not only for the organization, but for themselves. We assess their ability to handle the new position, especially their ability to handle it when we are ready to give it to them.

Over the years there are a variety of psychological tests that have been devised to help with these decisions. But, quite frankly, the tests are only partially successful. Not surprisingly, nothing replaces the experience and judgment of a seasoned executive.

Sometimes we place people in the wrong position, and, when it doesn't work out, have ourselves to blame as much as the person we promoted. I've been guilty of this and so have many of my clients, and we have all tried to learn from the few times it has occurred.

However, the most important lesson I learned was from my wife. Like many folks from Asia, she is short; she stands just slightly over five feet tall (about 1.5 meters) in her bare feet. To be honest, I don't often think about it, but one day I walked into our kitchen just in time to watch her pick up a long wooden spoon and use it to pull down some plastic bowls from the top cabinet in the kitchen.

I stood there amazed when she turned around and said "I do this all the time. You've just never been here to see it before. Getting the step ladder is too much trouble, and until we retire in the Philippines and I have a maid to help I had to devise a practical solution. It's why I put the plastic bowls and not the china and crystal on the top shelf."

"I've been able to overcome many shortcomings in my life, but I discovered very early that I would have to find a way to get around my height. I've done it by being aware and changing as much as I could, which includes putting the things I need the most in lower places and figuring out a way to get to the rest of the things that are beyond reach."

"You see, I learned how to spell and how to be polite; I learned how to read, write and speak several different languages, and I even learned how to paint watercolors to the point that I now call myself an artist. But, there was no way for me to learn how to be taller. It just isn't possible. So I've made adjustments. That's what you do in life."

It took a while before I really understood what she was telling me, but it's one of the most valuable lessons I've learned. Now, before I ask people to do things, I always make certain I'm not asking them to learn how to be taller.

Thanks for allowing me to share these stories. Feel free to share them with others.

ABOUT THE AUTHOR

John Fall is a senior global executive management leadership consultant, seminar/workshop facilitator, author and speaker. He has over four decades of experience with organizations ranging in size from a few hundred employees to hundreds of thousands worldwide. His clients include Honda, Toyota, General Motors, the Goodyear Tire and Rubber Company, Royal Dutch Shell, Australian Teleservices Association (ATA), IBM, Lockheed Martin, ESI International, Computer Task Group (ctg), and numerous small and mid-sized enterprises. His industry experience includes automotive, financial services, oil and gas, healthcare, employee benefits, mortgage banking, manufacturing, distribution, construction, real estate, insurance, and others.

Mr. Fall's consulting engagements -- predominantly initiated by client referrals -- have taken him throughout North America and Asia including Australia, Japan, the Philippines and Singapore.

Mr. Fall developed & conducted a seminar: "How to Implement an e-Business Strategy" for the Australian Teleservices Association (ATA), Sydney, Australia, created & conducted a Seminar/Workshop: "How to Select & Install Information Technology – a Management Perspective" for the International Foundation of Employee Benefit Plans Automation Institute, Palm Springs, California, and developed & delivered a speech to high school students: "What's Your Dream?" at the De La Salle-College of St. Benilde "Choose I.T.: Discover and Learn Your Future Conference" in Manila, Philippines.

Mr. Fall is listed in "Who's Who in the World", "Who's Who in America", "Who's Who in Finance and Industry", "Who's Who in Finance and Business", "Who's Who in Emerging Leaders in America", and "Who's Who in the West".

For further information, contact the author at jrfall@yahoo.com.

www.ingramcontent.com/pod-product-compliance
Lightning Source LLC
Chambersburg PA
CBHW051341170526
45166CB00002B/910